# ANNE FRANK
## A Life in Hiding

### by Wil Mara

**Content Consultant**
Nanci R. Vargus, Ed.D.
Professor Emeritus, University of Indianapolis

**Reading Consultant**
Jeanne M. Clidas, Ph.D.
Reading Specialist

**Children's Press®**
An Imprint of Scholastic Inc.

Library of Congress Cataloging-in-Publication Data

Names: Mara, Wil, author. | Shepherd, Jodie, author.
Title: Anne Frank : a life in hiding / by Wil Mara ; poem by Jodie Shepherd.
Description: [New York] : Children's Press, an imprint of Scholastic, Inc.,
[2016] | Series: Rookie biographies | Includes index.
Identifiers: LCCN 2015050832 | ISBN 9780531216828 (library binding) |
ISBN 9780531217641 (pbk.)
Subjects: LCSH: Frank, Anne, 1929-1945–Juvenile literature. | Jewish
children in the Holocaust–Netherlands–Amsterdam–Biography–Juvenile
literature. | Jews–Netherlands–Amsterdam–Biography–Juvenile
literature. | Amsterdam (Netherlands)–Biography–Juvenile literature.
Classification: LCC DS135.N6 F733927 2016 | DDC 940.53/18092–dc23
LC record available at http://lccn.loc.gov/2015050832

Produced by Spooky Cheetah Press
Poem by Jodie Shepherd

© 2017 by Scholastic Inc.

Printed in China 62

SCHOLASTIC, CHILDREN'S PRESS, ROOKIE BIOGRAPHIES™, and associated logos are
trademarks and/or registered trademarks of Scholastic Inc.

1 2 3 4 5 6 7 8 9 10 R 25 24 23 22 21 20 19 18 17 16

Photographs © : cover portrait: World History Archive/The Image Works; cover background, 3
background: AP Images; 4: United Archives GmbH/Alamy Images; 7: Anne Frank Fonds Basel/Getty
Images; 9: Fine Art Images/Superstock, Inc.; 10: Archive Photos/The Image Works; 11: Anne Frank
Fonds Basel/Getty Images; 12: Wim Wiskerke/Alamy Images; 15: Anne Frank Fonds Basel/Getty
Images; 16: Leo La Valle/Newscom; 17: AP Images; 19: Universal History Archive/Getty Images; 20-21:
Florian Bachmeier/Superstock, Inc.; 23: Superstock, Inc.; 24: Everett Historical/Shutterstock, Inc.; 27:
Calle Hesslefors/The Image Works; 29: World History Archive/The Image Works; 30 background:
AP Images; 31 top: Leo La Valle/Newscom; 31 center top: Florian Bachmeier/Superstock, Inc.; 31
center bottom: Fine Art Images/Superstock, Inc.; 31 bottom: Universal History Archive/Getty Images;
32 background: AP Images.

Maps by Mapping Specialists

# TABLE OF CONTENTS

4

# Meet Anne Frank

When she was 13 years old, Anne Frank had to go into hiding. Every day she poured her fears, hopes, and dreams into her diary. She died when she was just 15 years old. Yet Anne's voice continues to be heard. And her story continues to inspire.

Anne Frank was born on June 12, 1929, in Frankfurt, Germany. She had an older sister named Margot.

When Anne was a child, Germany was under the control of the **Nazis**. The Nazis were a political party led by Adolf Hitler.

**FAST FACT!**

Anne always liked to write. She dreamed of becoming a journalist.

This photo of Anne (left), her mother (middle), and sister (right) was taken in Germany. Anne was about four years old.

■Amsterdam
**NETHERLANDS**

**GERMANY**

●Frankfurt

## MAP KEY

● City where Anne
   Frank was born

■ City where Anne
   Frank lived

Area
enlarged

The Nazis treated **Jewish** people terribly. They stole their homes. They stole their businesses. They sent them to **concentration camps**. They even killed them outright. Anne's family was Jewish. They were not safe in Germany. In 1934, the family moved to the Netherlands.

Jewish people were made to wear this star on their clothing. "Jude" is German for "Jew."

By 1939, the Nazis started taking over other countries. This led to World War II. In May 1940, the Nazis took over the Netherlands. Once again, the Frank family was in danger.

There was one bright spot in Anne's life at this time. She was given a diary on her 13th birthday. She began writing in it every day.

This is a photo of Anne (left) and a friend taken in Amsterdam in 1940.

The Anne
Frank House

# Into the Annex

In 1942, Anne's family went into hiding. They moved into a secret **annex** in an office building. It was very small. The Franks had to be silent all day while people worked in the office. They could not go outside.

The place where the Franks lived is now a museum. It is called the Anne Frank House.

Soon four more people moved into the annex. They were Jewish, too. There were three adults and a teenage boy named Peter van Pels.

This made a tough situation even worse. Anne did not always get along with the adults. She was often hungry. There was not always enough food for everyone.

Peter van Pels became a good friend to Anne while they were in hiding.

Anne's bedroom and writing desk are re-created at the Anne Frank Museum.

Anne found comfort by writing in her diary. She wrote about the difficulties of living with so many people. She wrote about her growing friendship with Peter. She wrote about her anger toward the Nazis. But she also wrote about her hope— and belief—that good would win over evil.

Pages from Anne's diary

# Caught!

On August 4, 1944, tragedy struck the Frank family. Nazi police found the people hiding in the annex. Everyone was arrested and sent to concentration camps. In the confusion, Anne's diary was left on the floor, forgotten.

## FAST FACT!

History experts still do not know who told the Nazis about the Franks and where they were hiding.

Nazi police round up Jews to send them to concentration camps.

The Franks arrived at the Auschwitz concentration camp on September 6, 1944. As soon as they arrived, the family was split up. Anne and Margot went with their mother. Their father was led away. Anne would never see him again.

This is Auschwitz, the camp where the Frank family was first sent.

21

Many children were killed as soon they reached the camps. The men in charge almost sent Anne to her death. Then they decided she was strong enough to work.

Anne and the other prisoners worked very hard all day long. There was very little food in the camp. Rats and mice ran everywhere. A lot of prisoners were sick with disease.

Anne was just 15 years old when she arrived at Auschwitz.

This photo shows a group of prisoners at a concentration camp.

In October, Anne and Margot were moved to a camp called Bergen-Belsen. Their mother was not allowed to go with them. She died in Auschwitz in January 1945.

Anne and her sister became very sick. They had a disease called typhus (TIE-fuss). They died in February 1945. Within months, the Nazis were defeated. All the prisoners were set free.

# A Voice Never Silenced

The only member of Anne's family left alive in 1945 was her father, Otto. All the other people who lived in the annex had been killed.

Otto Frank found Anne's diary. He had it made into a book. It is called *The Diary of a Young Girl*. The book became a best seller.

This photo of Otto Frank was taken in 1976.

Anne Frank showed how war destroys lives. But she also showed how some people can still live and hope and dream—no matter how bad things may seem.

# Timeline of Anne Frank's Life

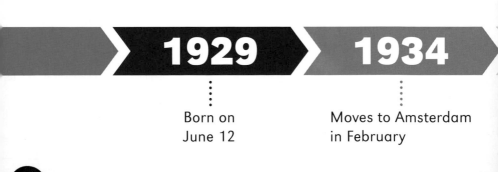

**1929**
Born on
June 12

**1934**
Moves to Amsterdam
in February

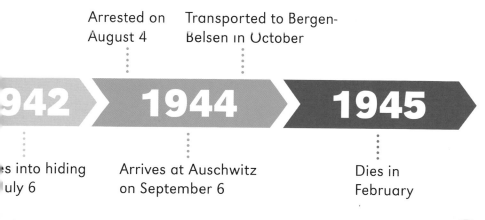

Arrested on
August 4

Transported to Bergen-
Belsen in October

**942**

**1944**

**1945**

...s into hiding
...uly 6

Arrives at Auschwitz
on September 6

Dies in
February

# A Poem About Anne Frank

For no reason but that her family was Jewish,
Anne hid in an annex for year after year.
Her life was cut short, but because of her diary
Her story and voice will always ring clear.

# You Can Be Inspiring

Find ways to express yourself.

Do not ever lose hope—even when life is most difficult.

Try to find the positive in every situation.

# Glossary

- **annex** (AN-eks): smaller building that is connected to a main building

- **concentration camps** (KAHN-suhn-tray-shun KAMPS): places where Nazis' prisoners were sent

- **Jewish** (JOO-ish): relating to a person whose religion is Judaism

- **Nazis** (NAHT-seez): members of a political group that ruled Germany from 1933 to 1945

# Index

# Facts for Now

Visit this Scholastic Web site for more information on Anne Frank:
**www.factsfornow.scholastic.com**
Enter the keywords Anne Frank

# About the Author

**Wil Mara** has been intrigued by Anne Frank since reading *The Diary of a Young Girl* in his freshman year of high school. He is a best-selling and award-winning author of more than 150 books, many of which are educational titles for children.